Coloring with *BellaLee*

By Sasha Dixon

Illustrated by Skyler Warren

Sasha S. Dixon, author and artist,
from Cleveland Heights, OH.
Graduate of The University Of Akron.
Author of *123 with Bella Lee, Let's explore our
ABC's with Bella Lee and Colors with Bella Lee; Charm & Passion*
developed a love for education after becoming a mother.
Email - sasha.dixon.sd@gmail.com
Facebook - @sashadixon19
Twitter - @SashaDixon19
Instagram - @sashadixon19

This publication is dedicated to Bella Lee
and Dr. Martin Luther King Jr.

Skyler S. Warren, Multi Media Artist
Graduate of The University Of Akron
Illustrator of the cover of *Charm & Passion;*
Illustrator for *123 with Bella lee, Lets explore our ABC's with Bella Lee,
and Colors with Bella Lee.* Skyler finds passion in working as a
Graphic designer bringing the life to new ideas.
Helping others while creating smiles wherever he goes.
Email: skylerswarren@gmail.com
Website: http://www.psbsstudios.com
YoutubeChannel: Powersketchbysky

ISBN 979-8-218-00827-7
Library of Congress Control Number:

Printed in the United States of America 2022

Primary Colors

(prahy-mer-eekuhl-ers)

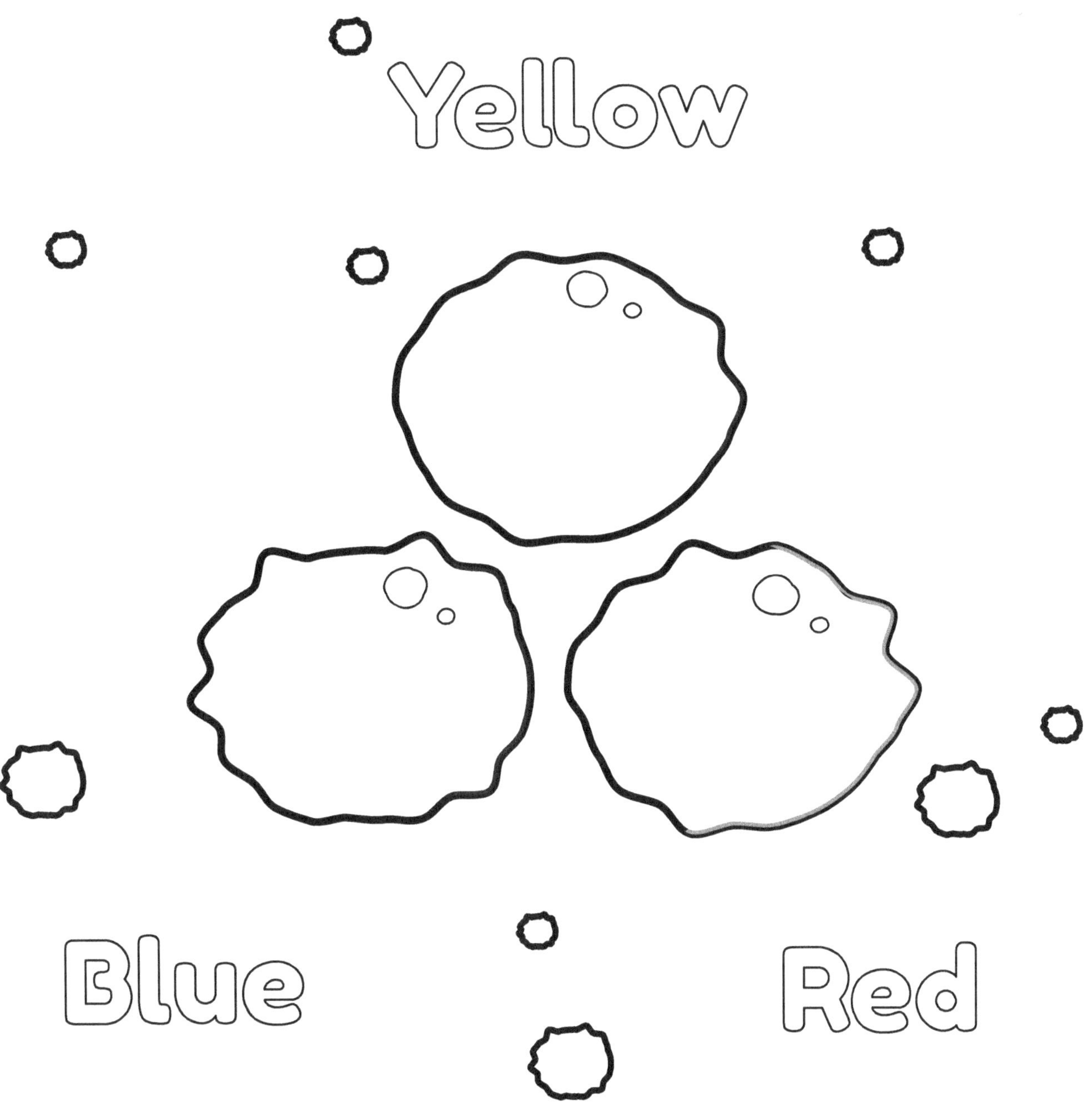

A primary color is a color that cannot be made from a combination of any other colors. There are three primary colors blue, yellow and red. These three colors are hues that in theory can be mixed to make all other colors. A hue is the specific look or pigment of a color.

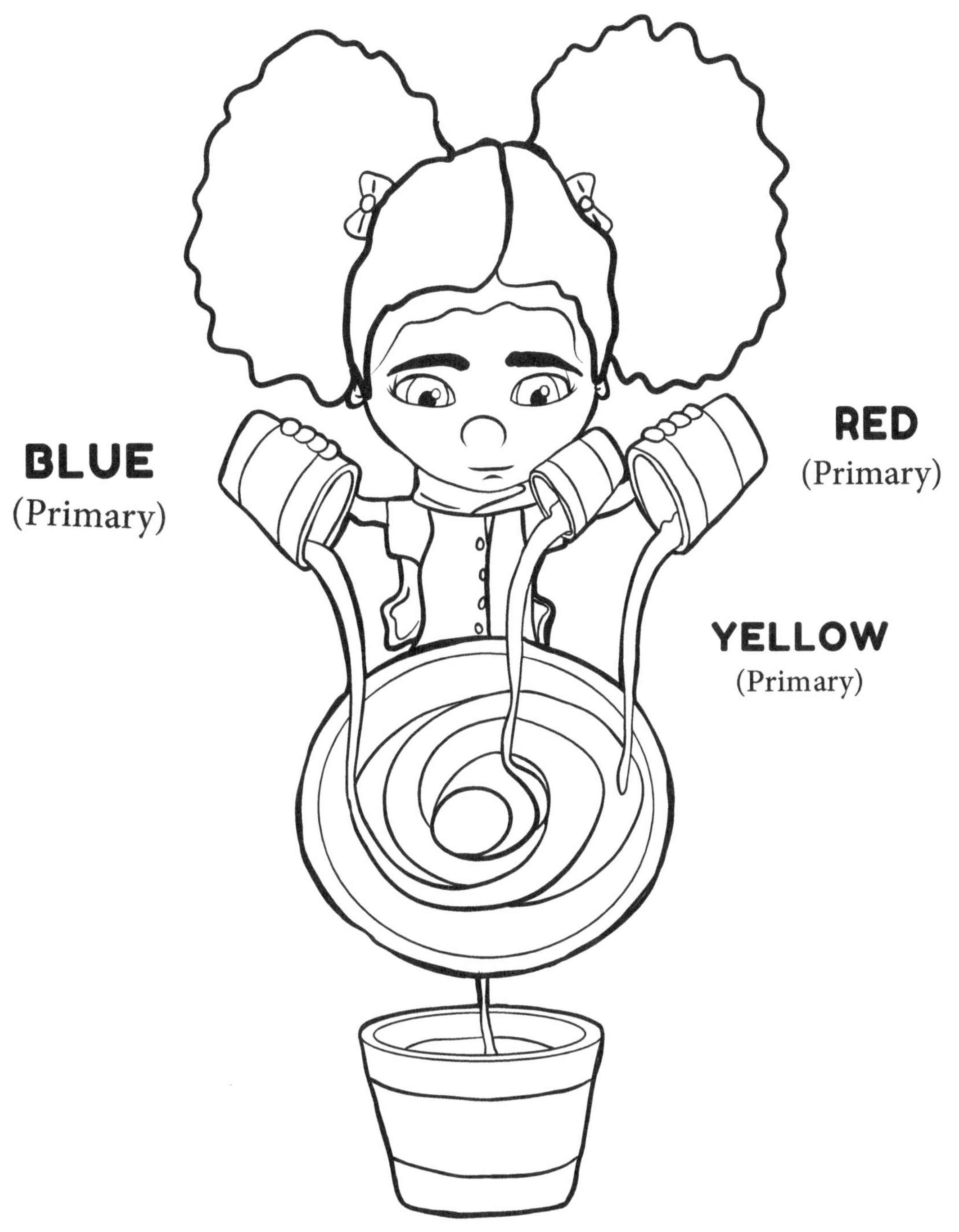

If you mix three primary colors blue, yellow and red.
In theory it will produce black.

This is a red apple.

These are the words, red apple.

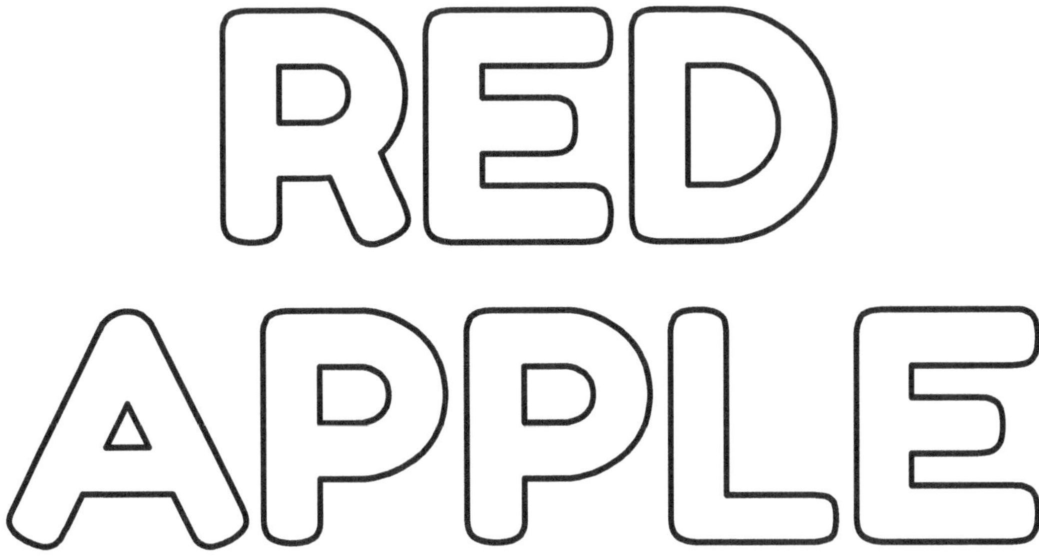

Bella is driving a red car.

This is a blue fish.

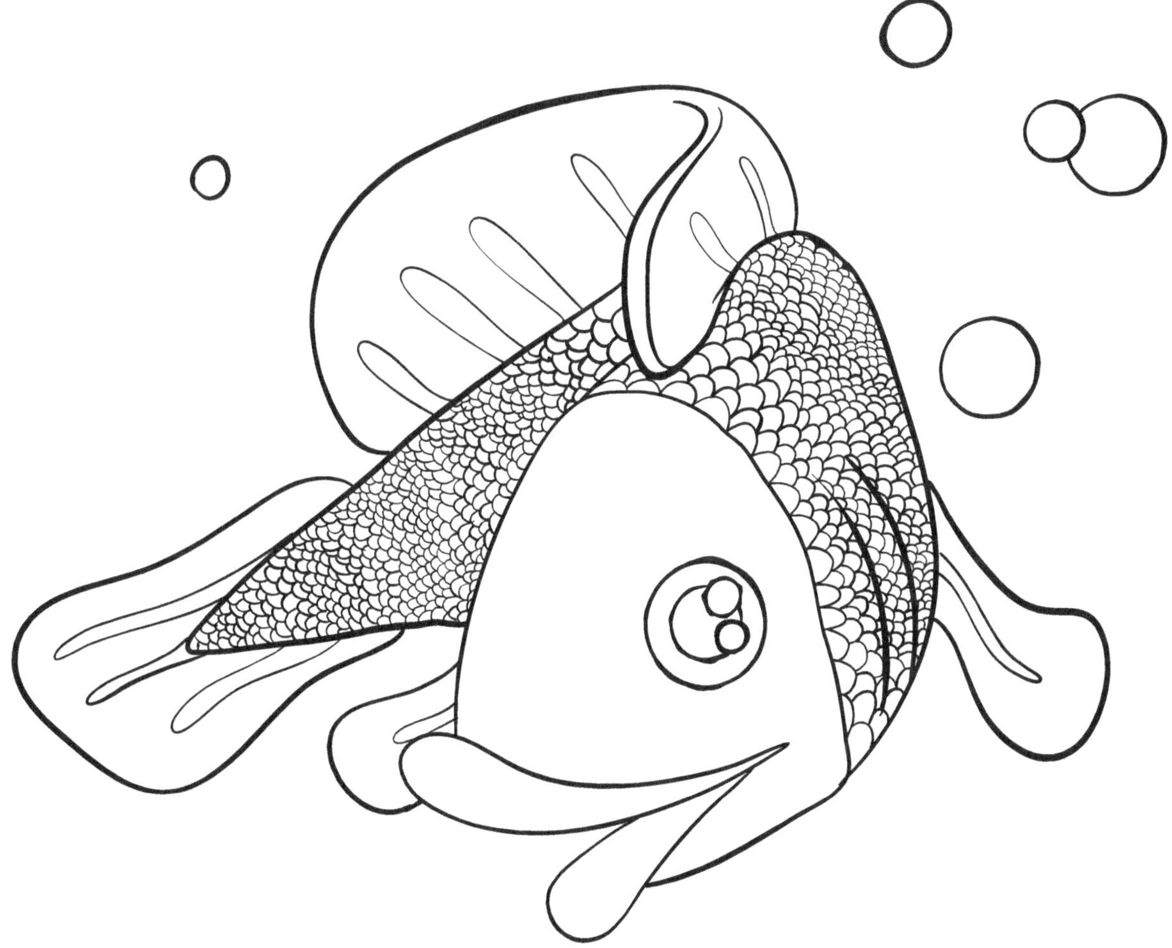

These are the words, blue fish.

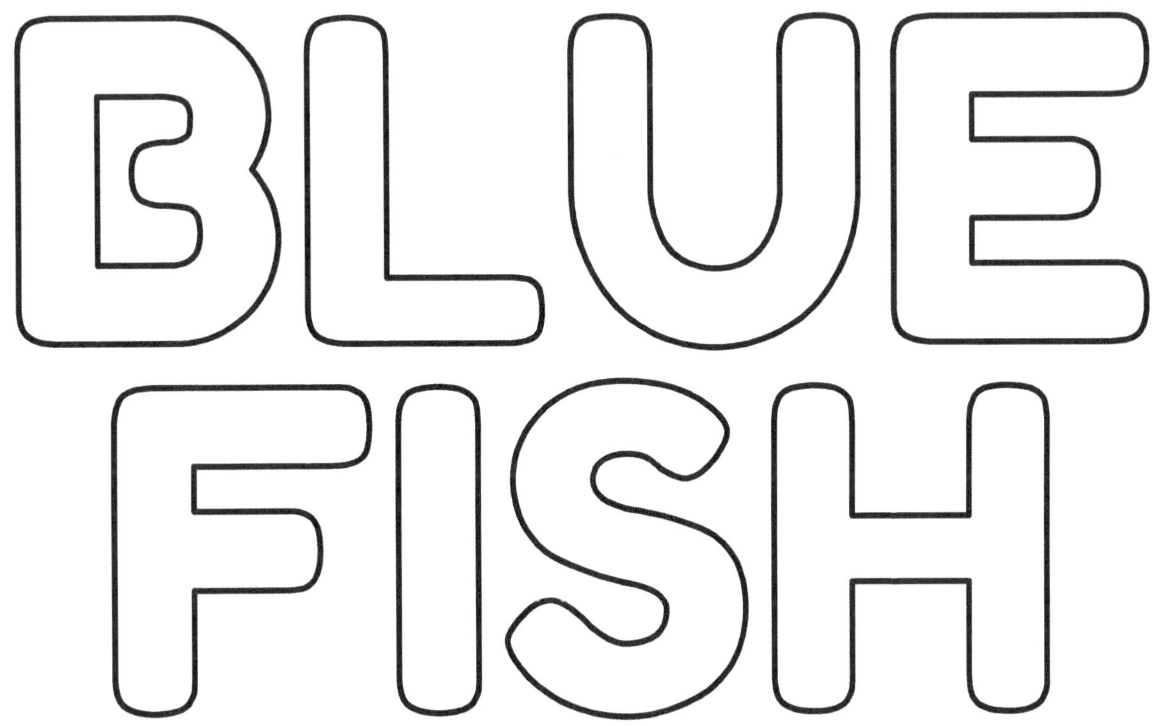

Bella is painting a blue fish.

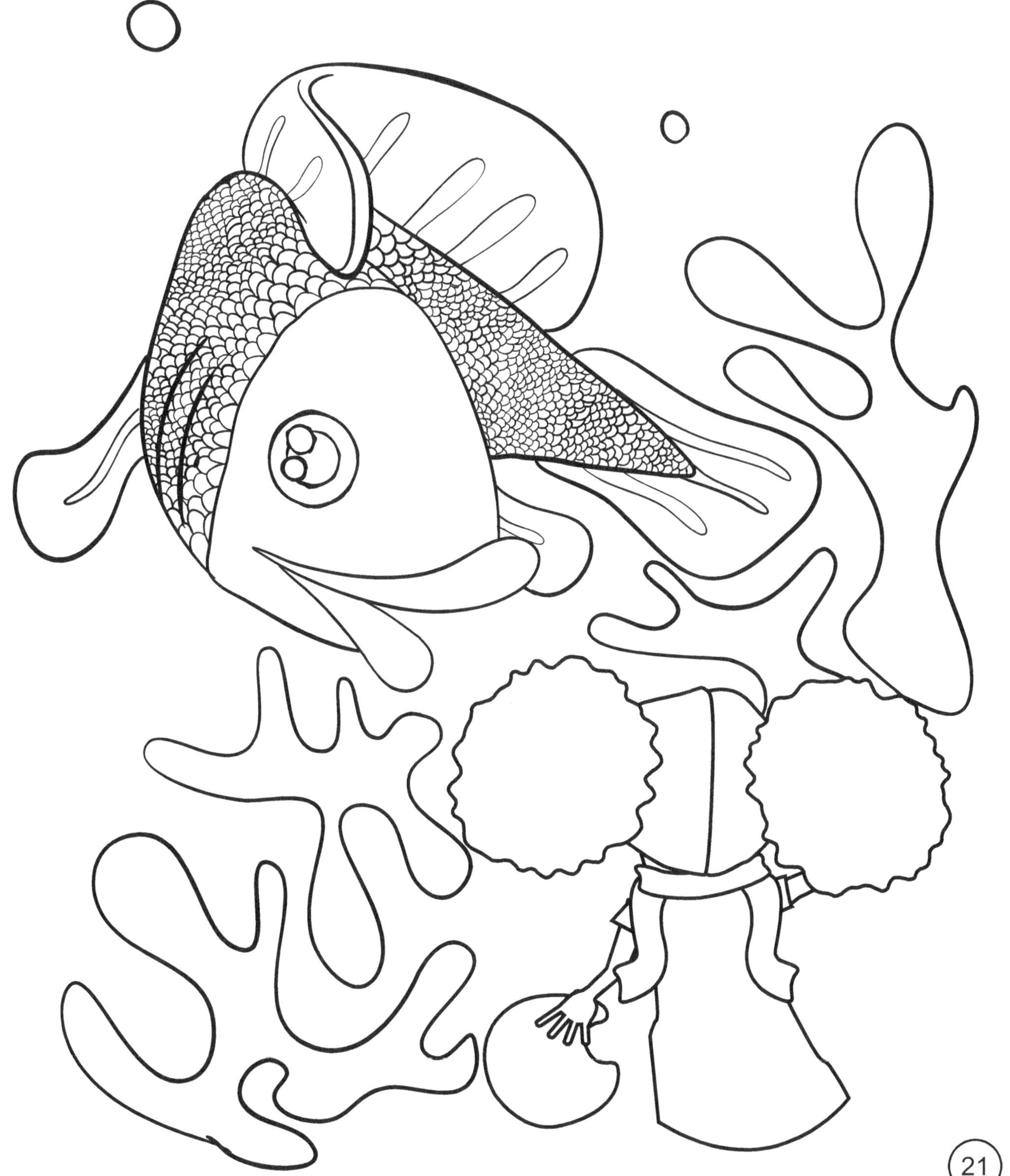

21

This is a yellow sun.

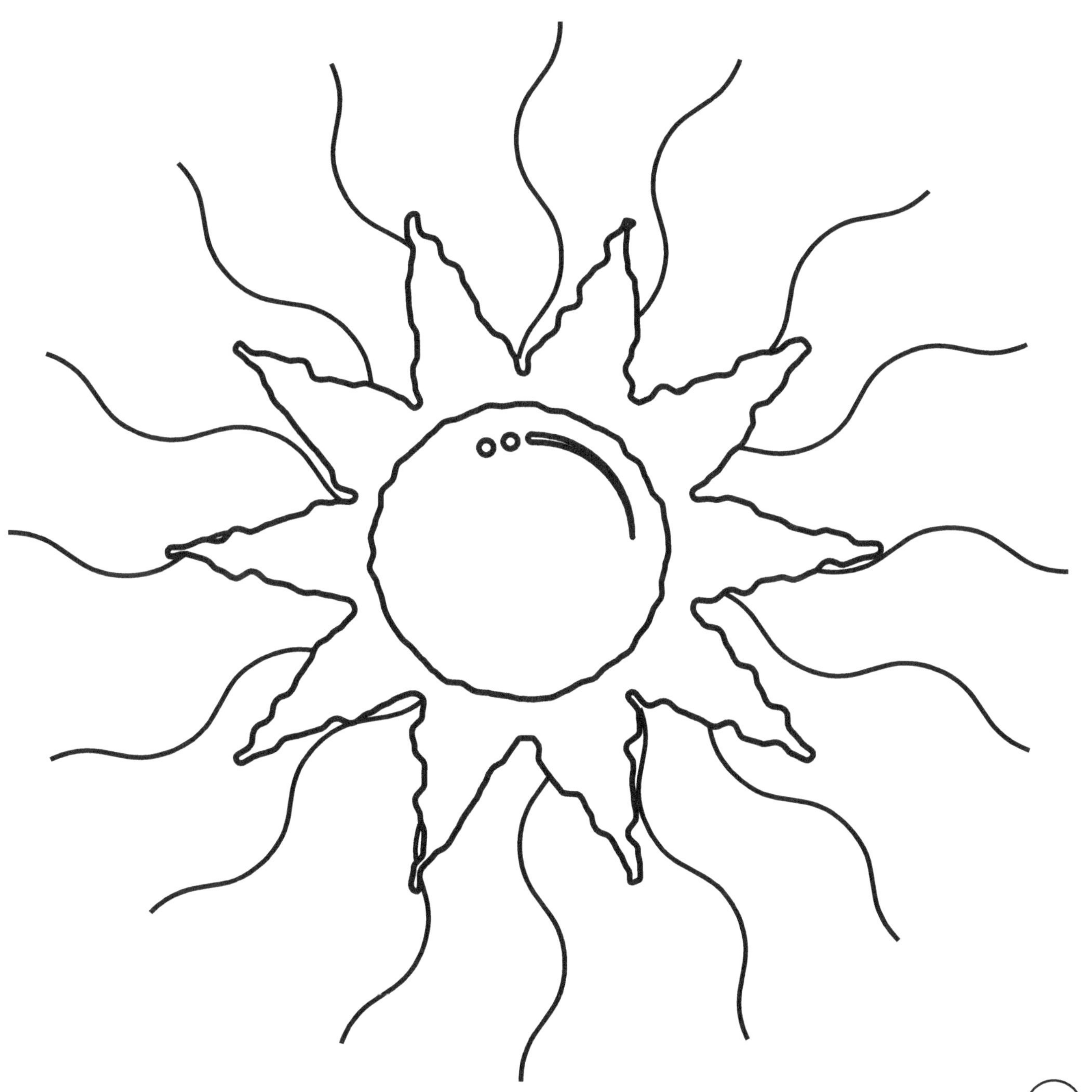

These are the words, yellow sun.

YELLOW
SUN

Bella saw a yellow bus,
during the season of spring.

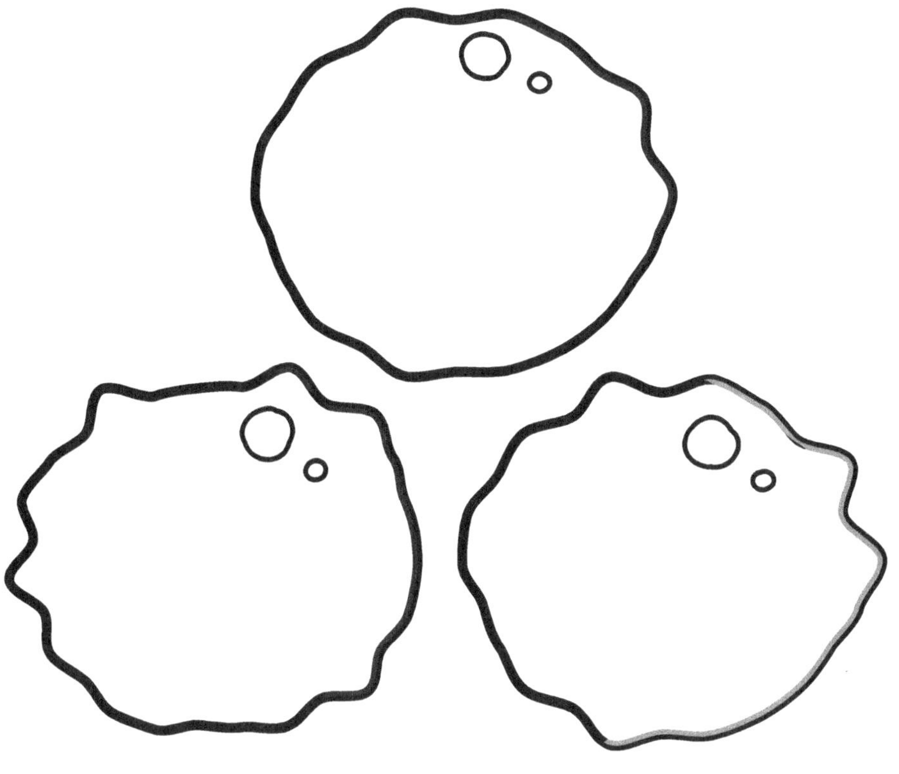

Secondary Colors

(sek-uhn-der-eekuhl-ers)

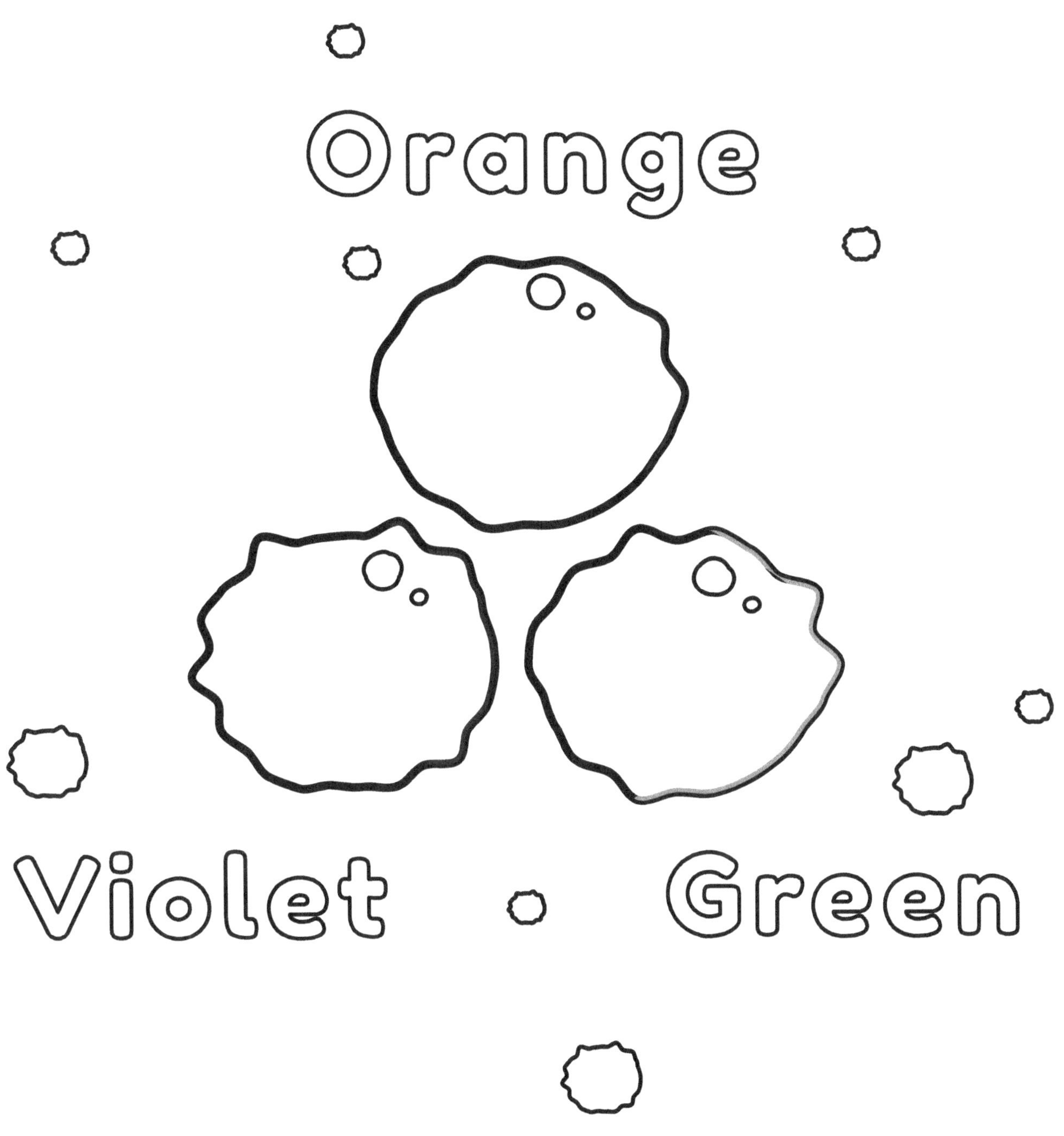

There are three secondary colors violet, orange, and green. By mixing two primary hues together you will produce a secondary color.

By mixing red and blue together you will create the color violet.

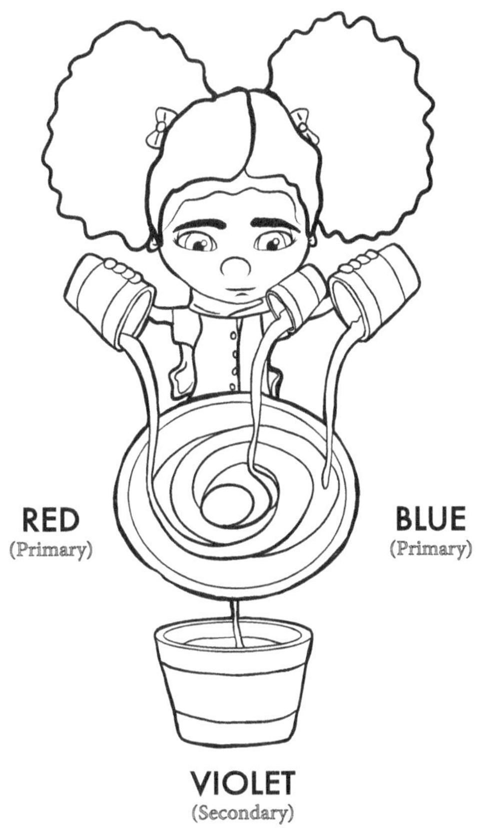

By mixing red and yellow together you will create the color orange.

By mixing yellow and blue
together you will create
the color green.

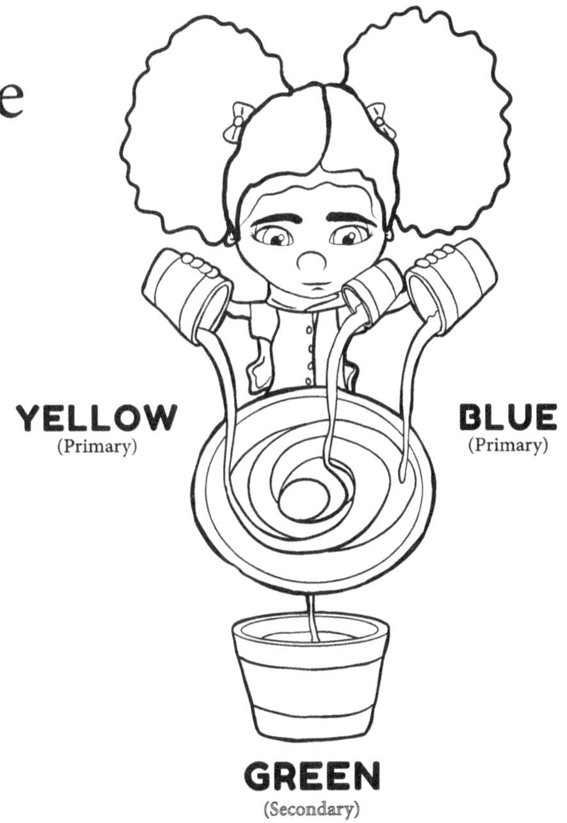

This is a orange pumpkin.

These are the words, orange pumpkin.

ORANGE
PUMPKIN

Bella is picking a big orange pumpkin for her Halloween costume this year.

This is a violet shoe.

These are the words, violet shoe.

Bella is wearing her violet shoes at her concert with the chickadee choir.

This is a green leaf.

These are the words, green leaf.

Bella is watching the green leaves fall from the tree.

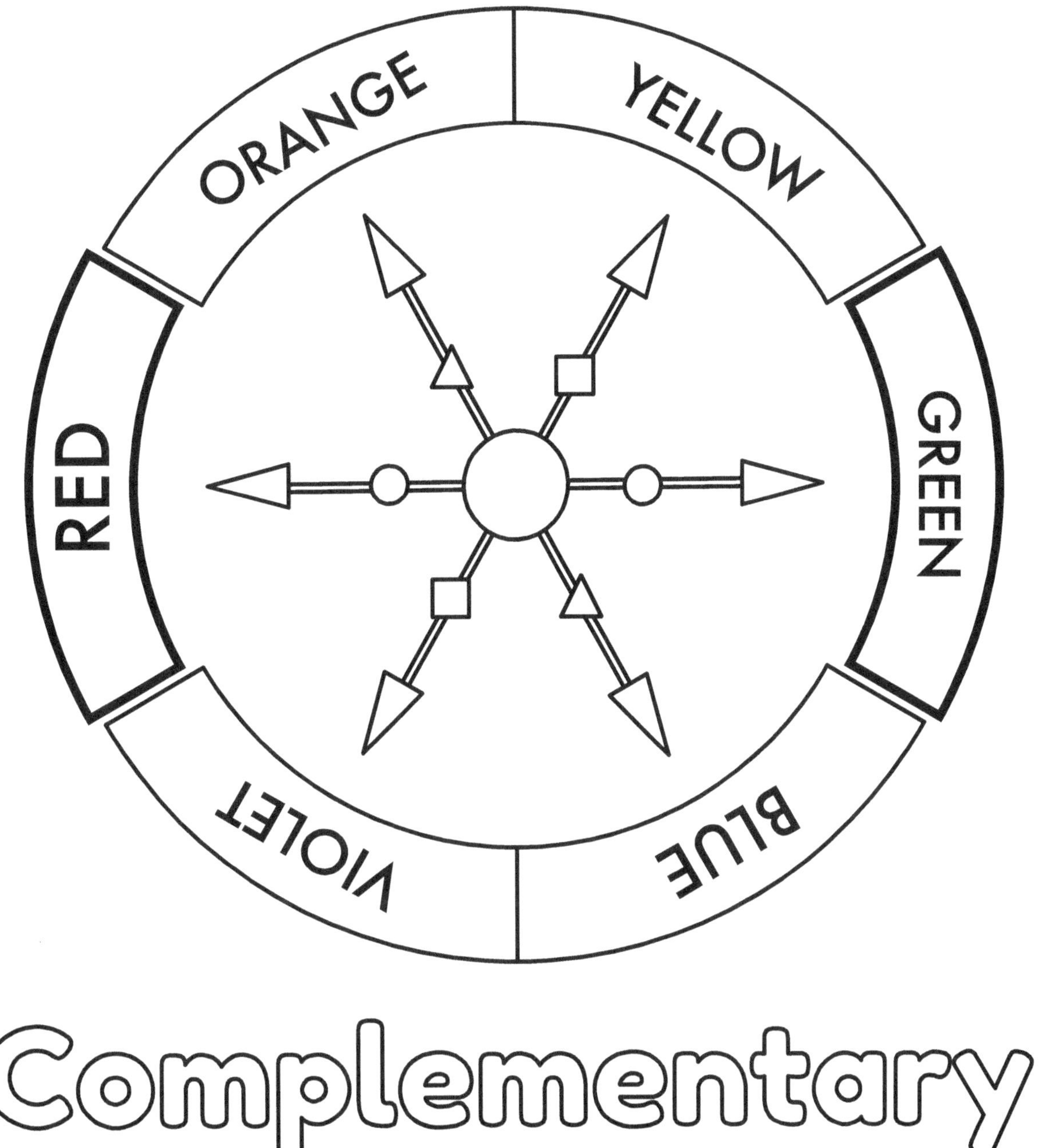

Complementary
Colors

Complementary colors are colors that are opposite of each other on the color wheel. Complementary colors complement each other.

This is an example of a color wheel that displays complementary colors.

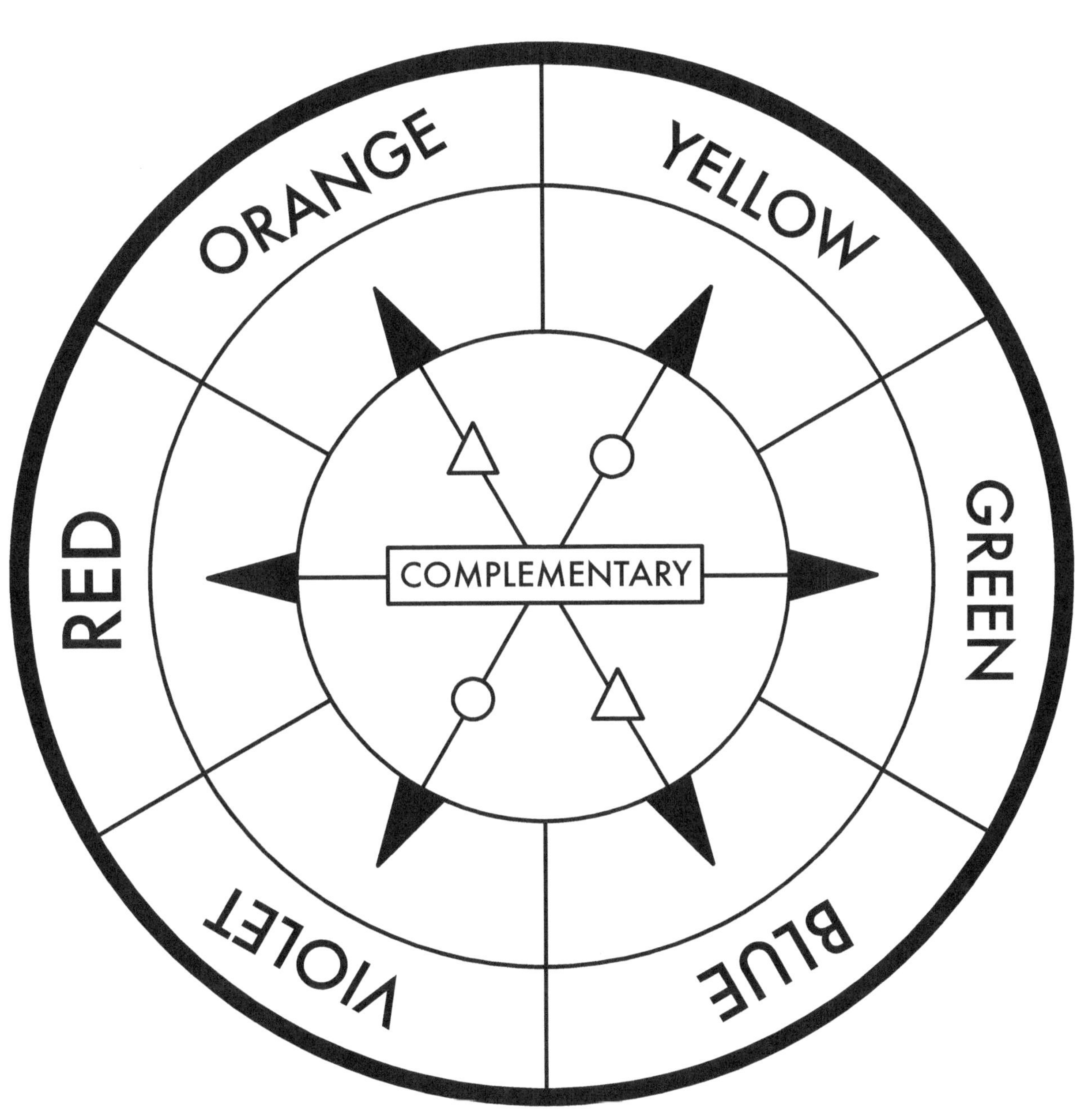

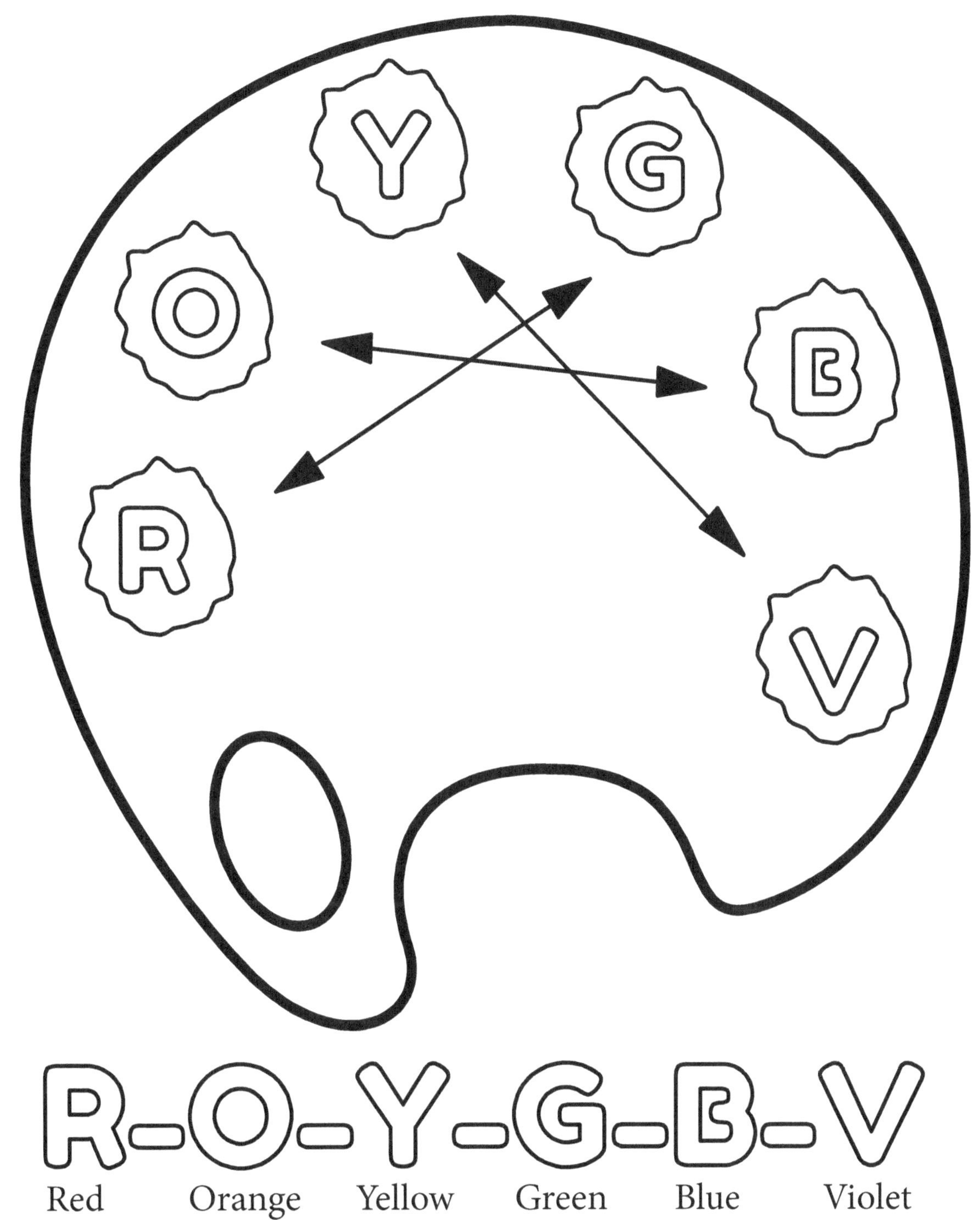

R-O-Y-G-B-V

Red Orange Yellow Green Blue Violet

R-O-Y-G-B-V is a great way to remember your primary colors. Also, it is the order in which artist prepare colors to paint on their paint palette.

Red and green are colors that complement one another. Look at little Bella, putting a red candy cane on a green Christmas tree.

Orange and blue are colors that complement each other. Bella is looking at her reflection in the shiny blue and orange Christmas ornament.

You are very pretty.
Yellow and violet are colors
that compliment one another.
I like your stripes!

The yellow bee is dancing
with the violet flower.
You smell nice.
you're a great
dancer.

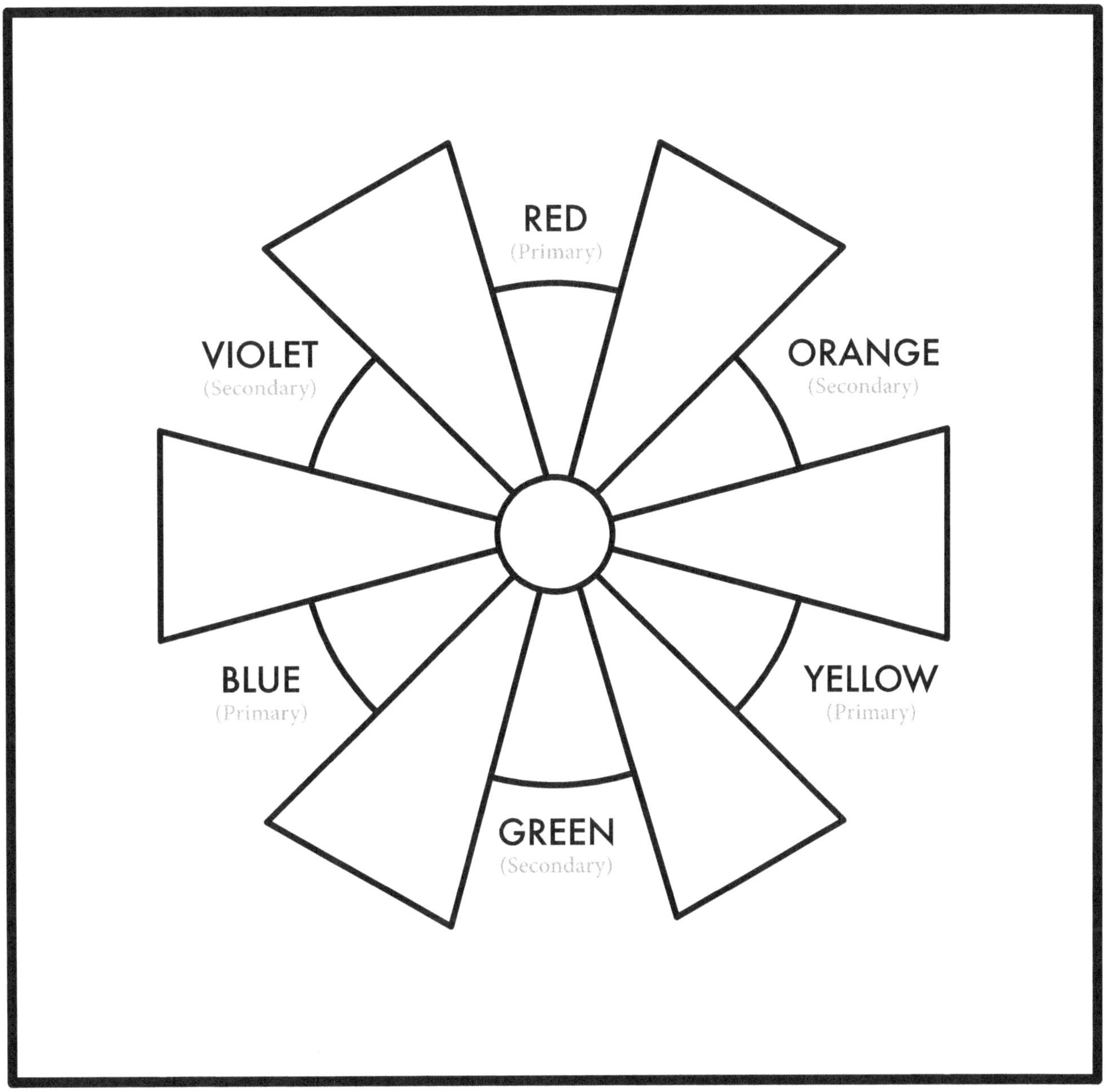

Tertiary
(tur-shee-er-ee)

Tertiary colors are made by mixing a primary color and a secondary color together.

By mixing red and violet together you will create the color red-violet.

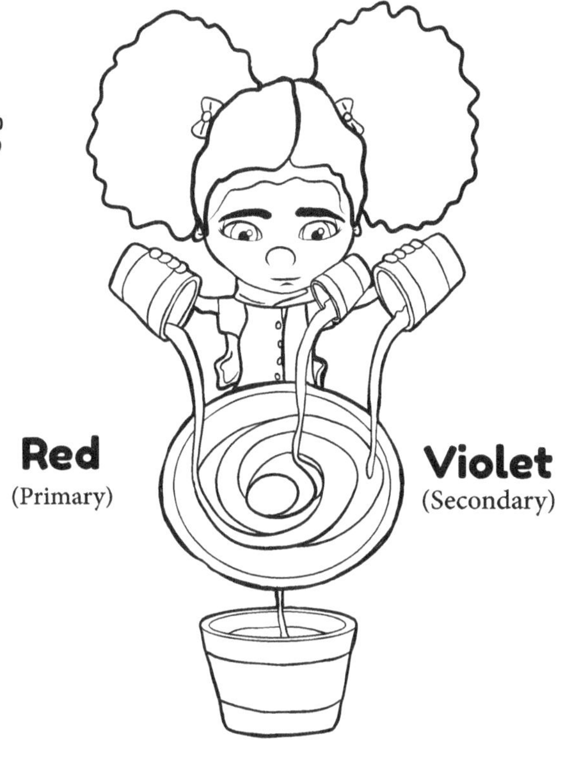

By mixing red and orange together you will create the color red-orange.

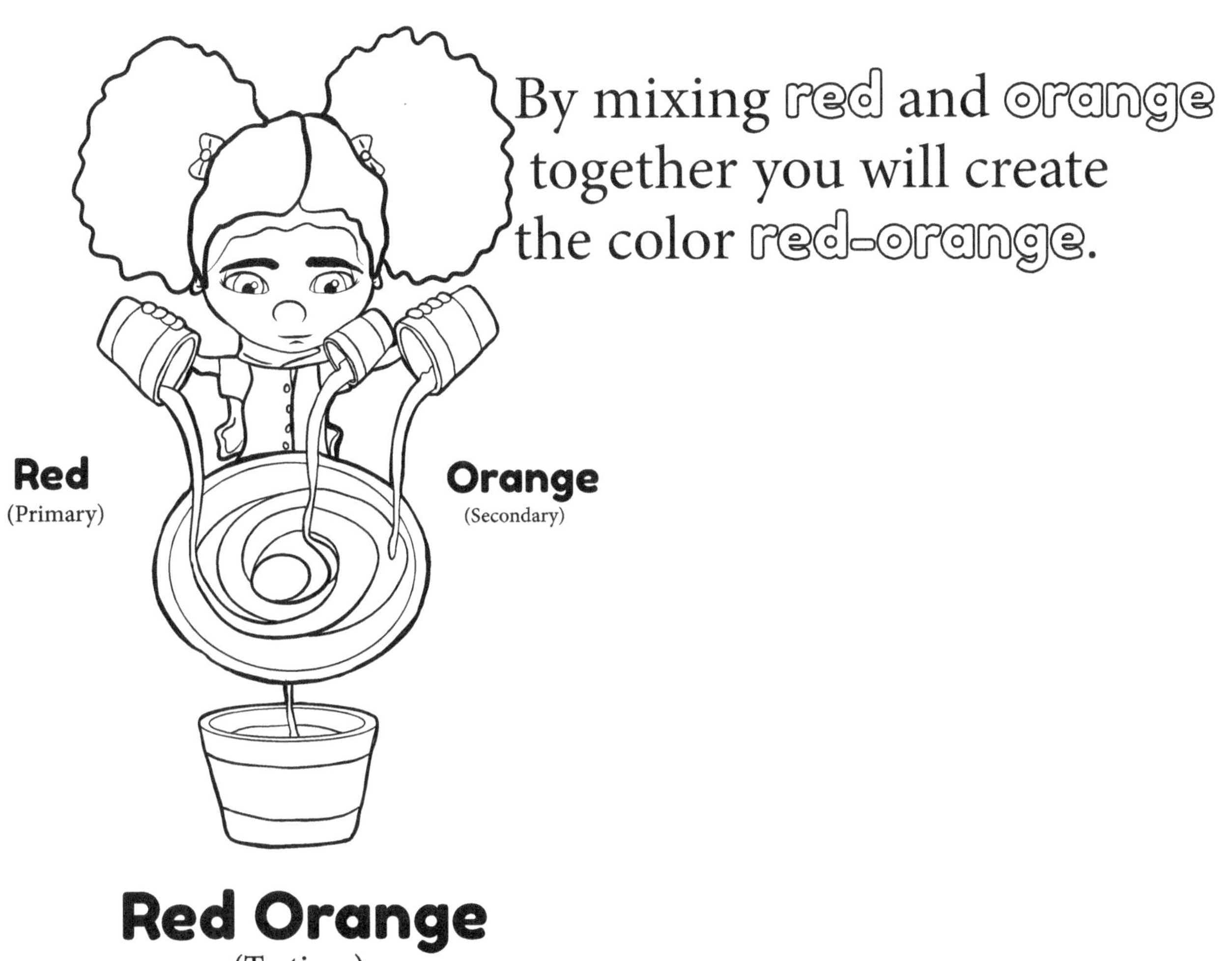

By mixing yellow and orange
together you will create
the color yellow-orange.

Yellow Orange
(Tertiary)

By mixing blue and violet together you will create the color blue-violet.

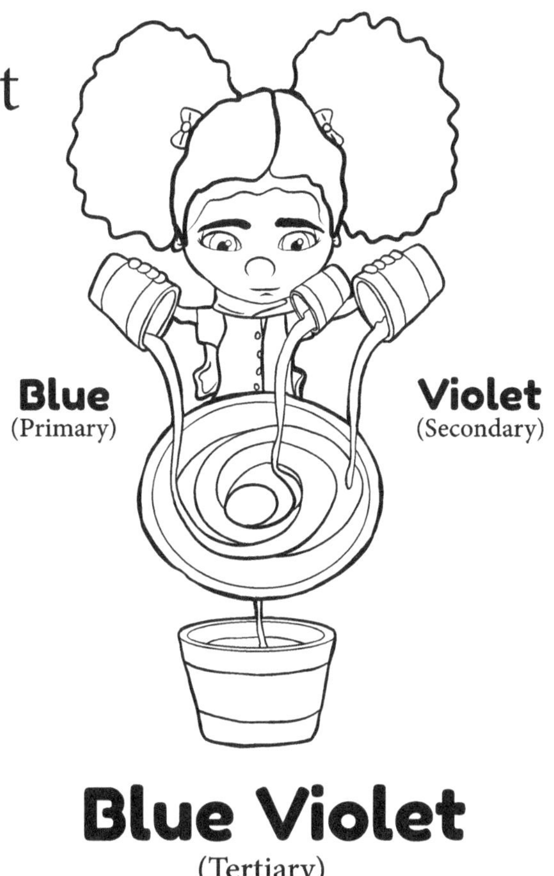

Blue Violet
(Tertiary)

By mixing yellow and green together you will create the color yellow-green.

By mixing blue and green together you will create the color blue-green.

Blue Green

(Tertiary)

This is a red-orange crayon.

This is a **blue-violet** crayon.

This is a yellow-orange crayon.

This is a red-violet crayon.

This is a yellow-green crayon.

Let's Color Again

Recommendations:
123 with BellaLee,
Lets explore our ABC's with BellaLee.
Colors with Bella Lee

Let's Count to Ten!

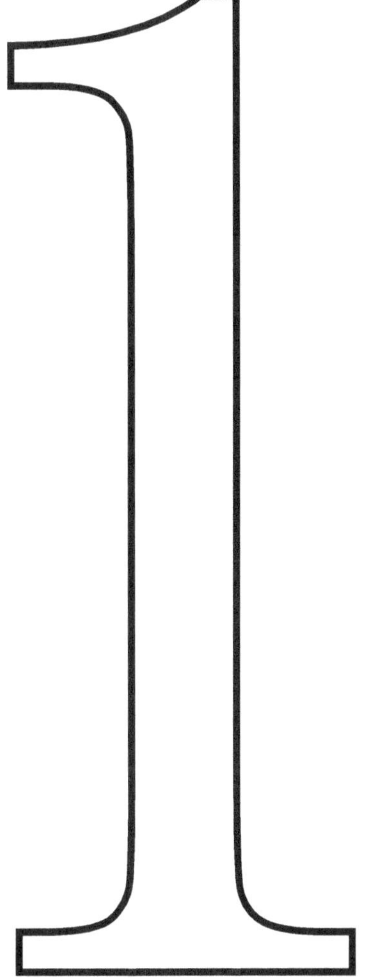

THIS IS THE NUMBER **ONE!**

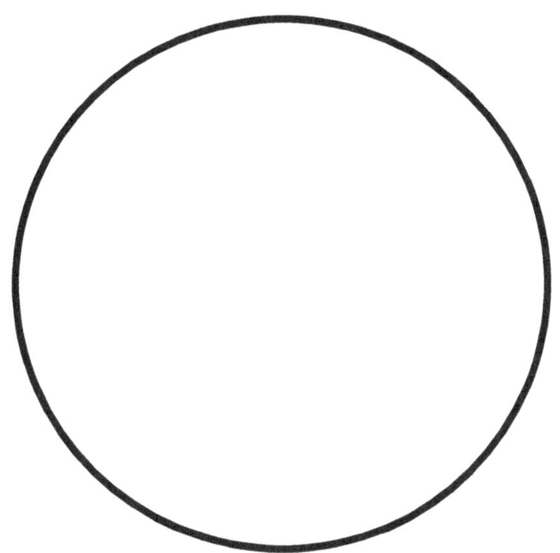

THIS IS **ONE** CIRCLE!

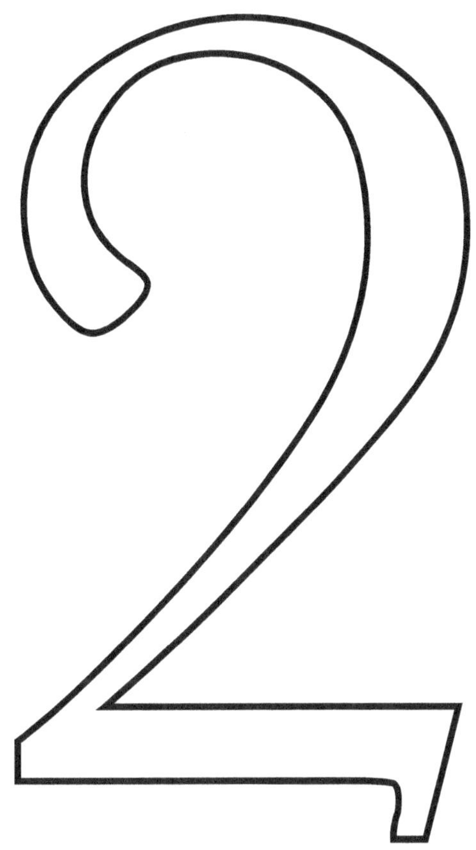

THIS IS THE NUMBER **TWO!**

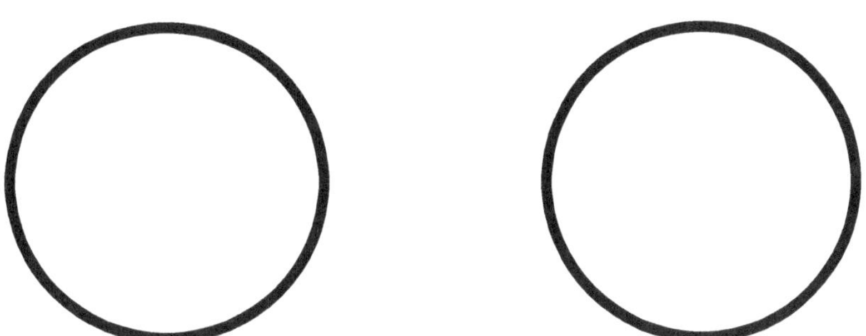

HERE ARE **TWO** CIRCLES!

THIS IS THE NUMBER **THREE!**

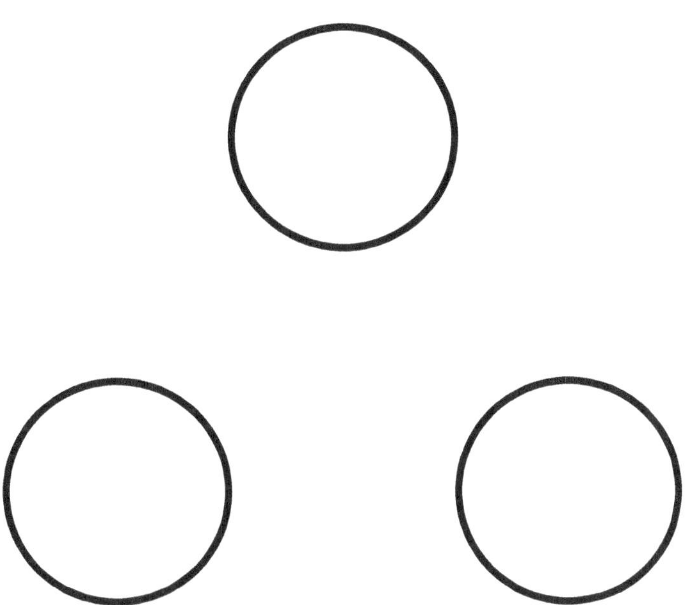

HERE ARE **THREE** CIRCLES!

THIS IS THE NUMBER **FOUR!**

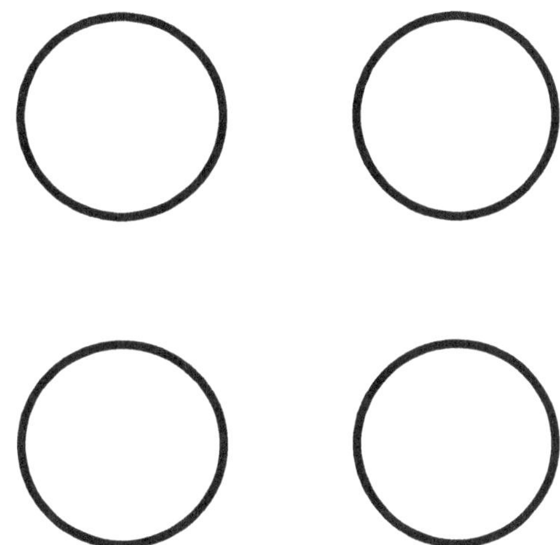

HERE ARE **FOUR** CIRCLES!

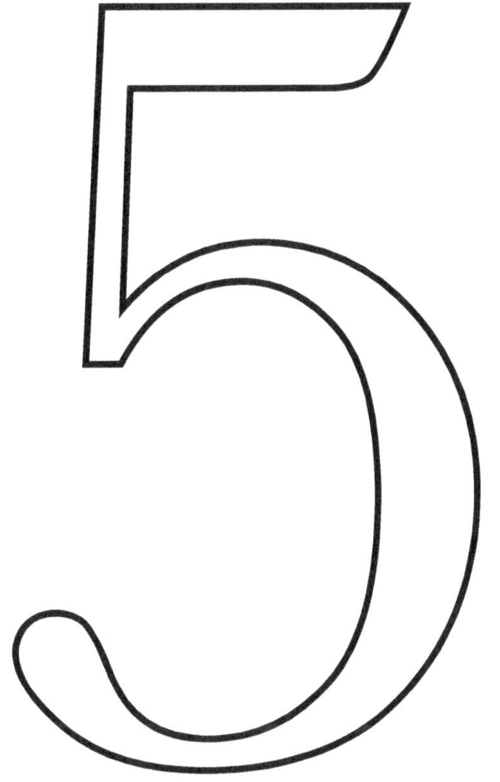

THIS IS THE NUMBER **FIVE!**

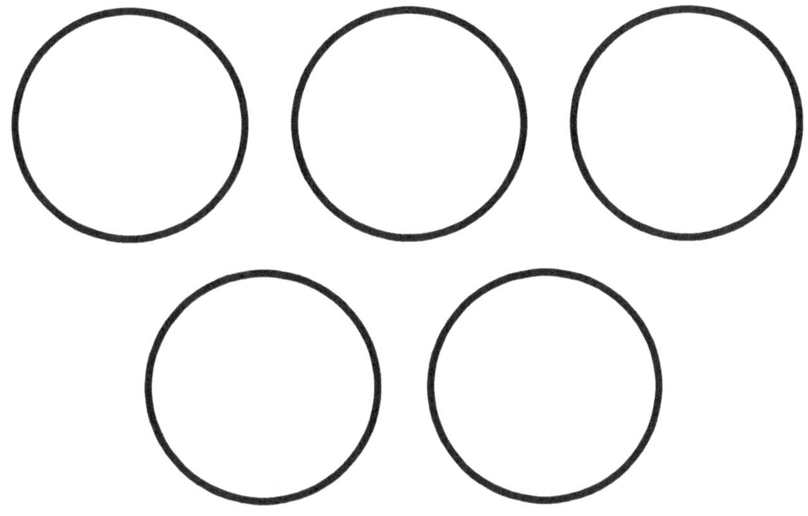

HERE ARE **FIVE** CIRCLES!

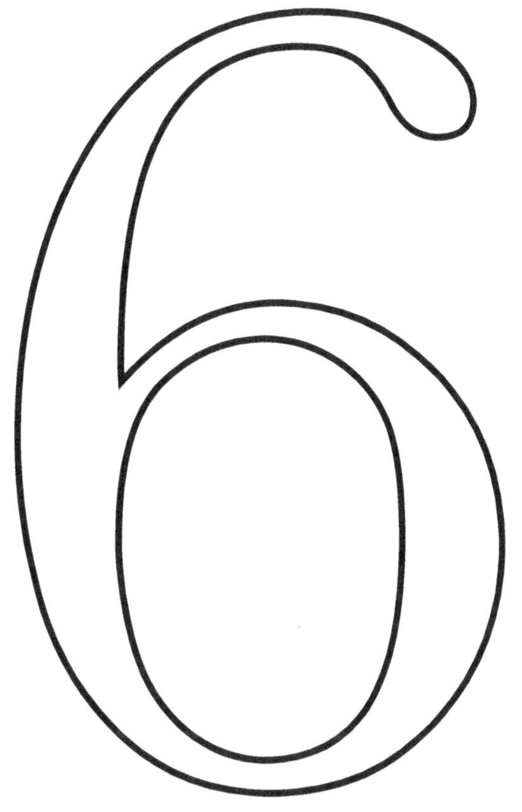

THIS IS THE NUMBER **SIX!**

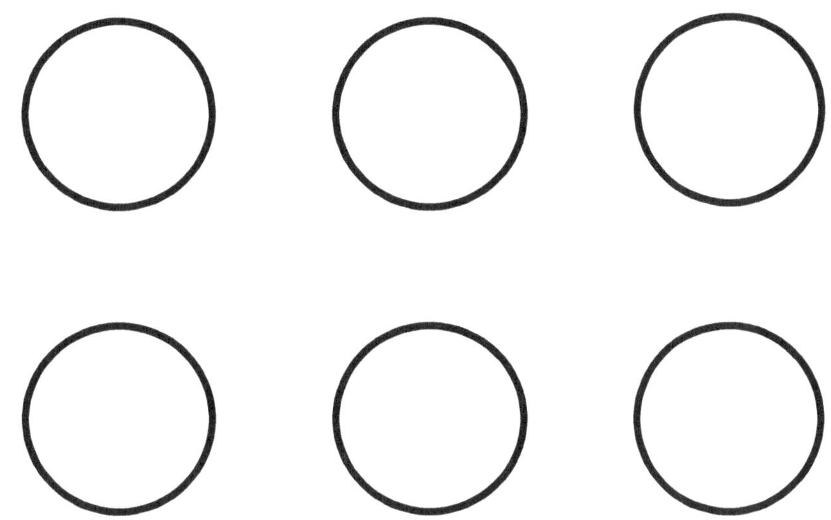

HERE ARE **SIX** CIRCLES!

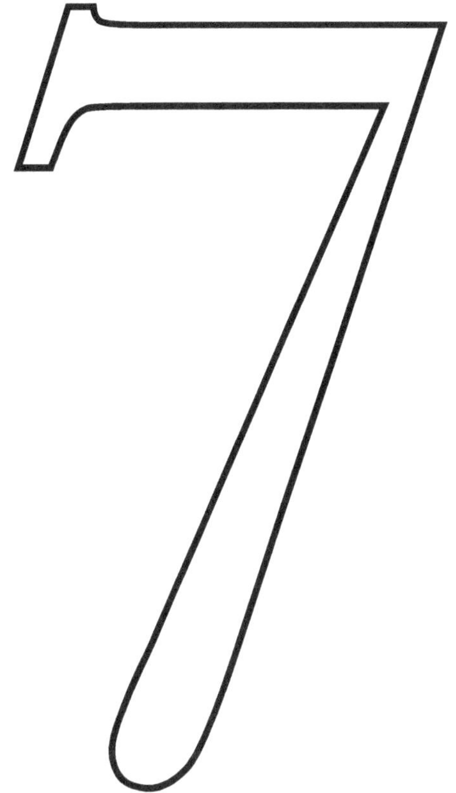

THIS IS THE NUMBER **SEVEN!**

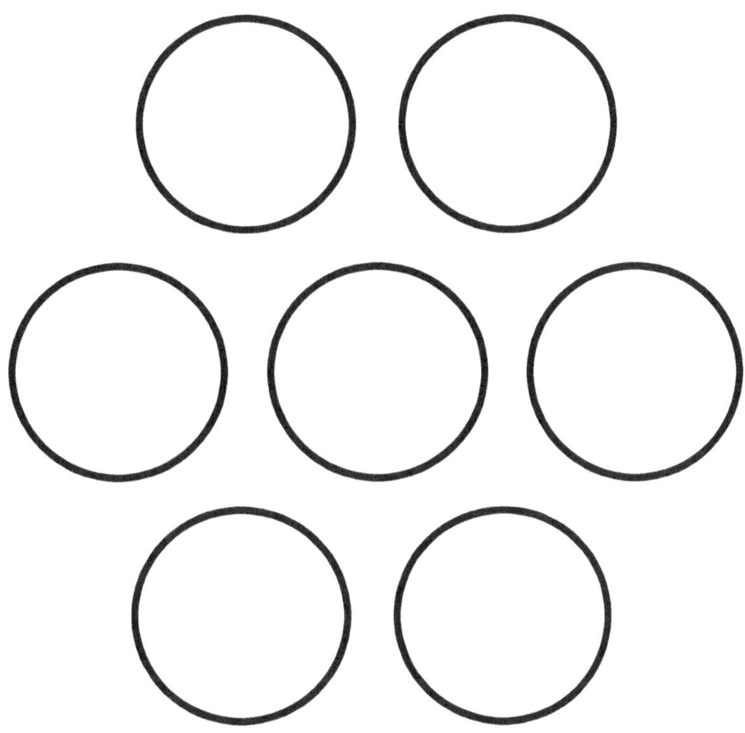

HERE ARE **SEVEN** CIRCLES!

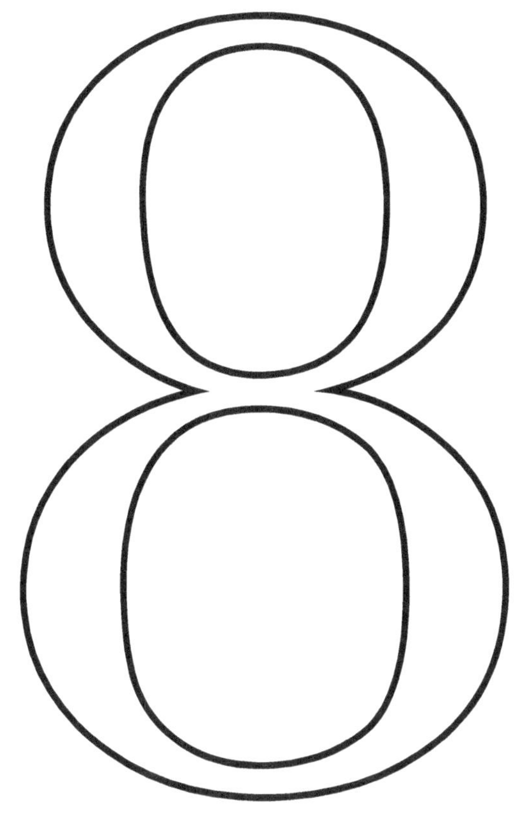

THIS IS THE NUMBER **EIGHT!**

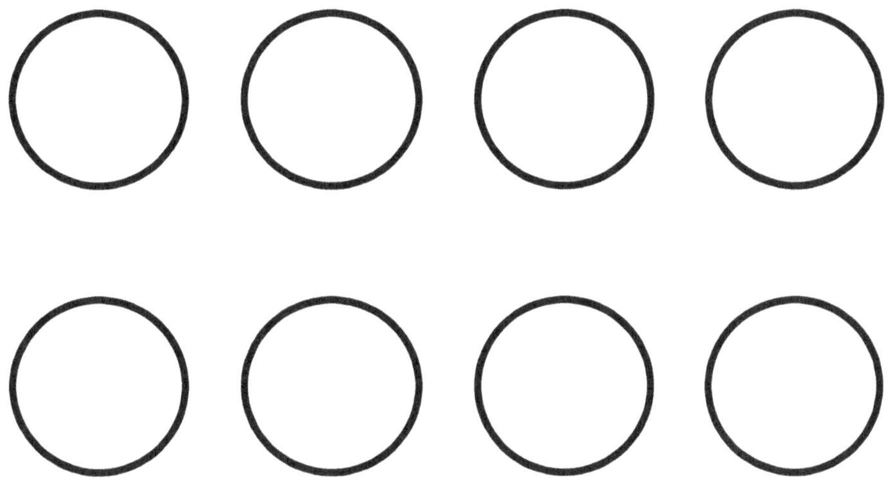

HERE ARE **EIGHT** CIRCLES!

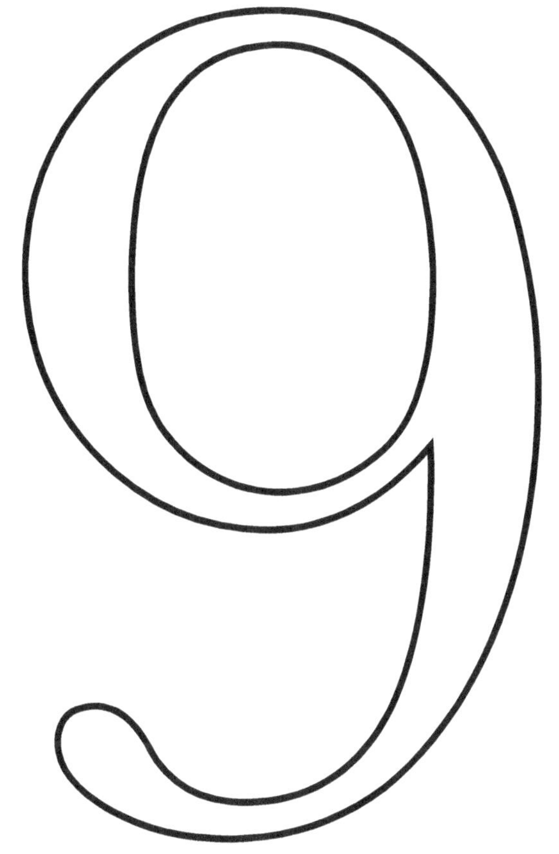

THIS IS THE NUMBER **NINE!**

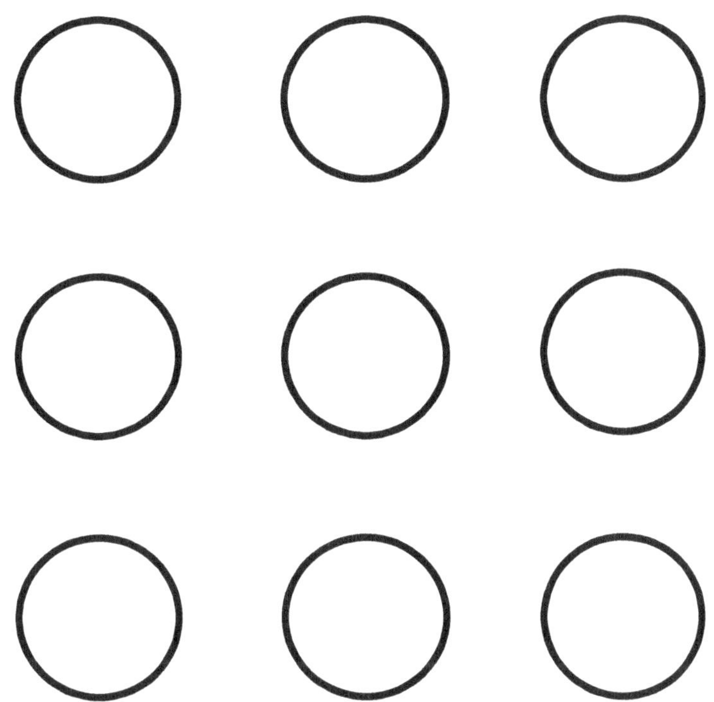

HERE ARE **NINE** CIRCLES!

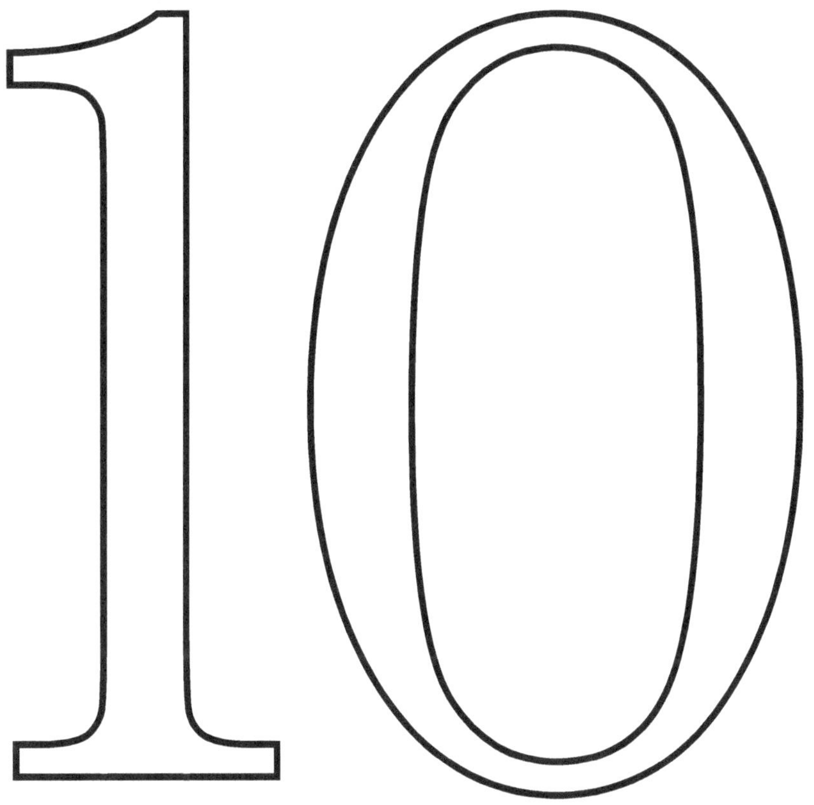

THIS IS THE NUMBER **TEN!**

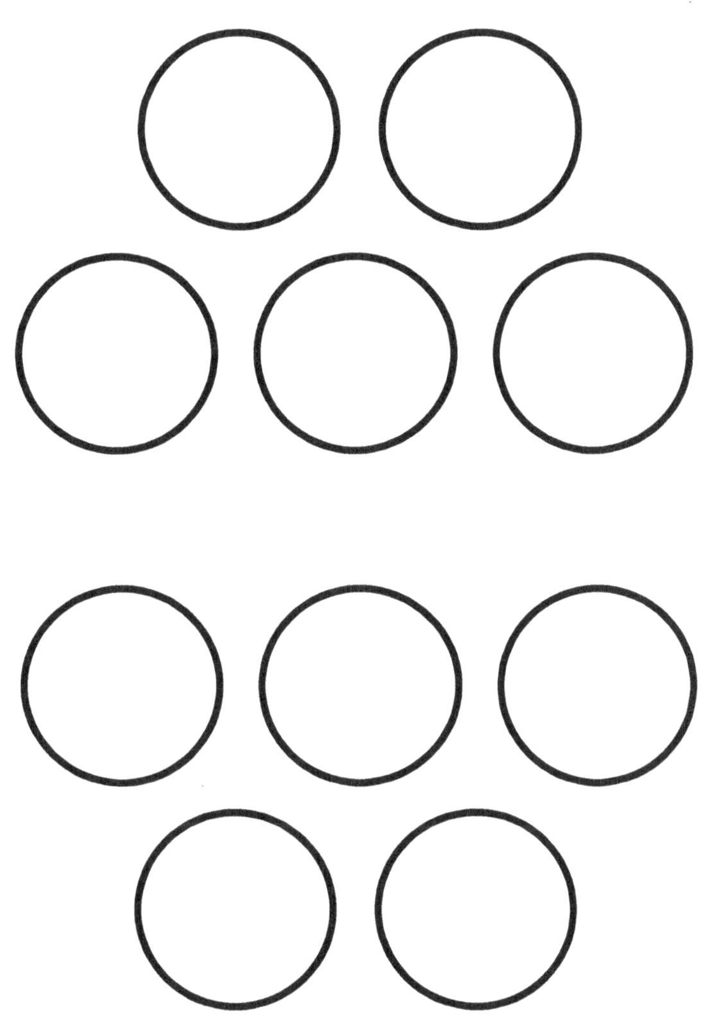

HERE ARE **TEN** CIRCLES!